Table of Contents

About the Author

Dmitry Bogomazov is a 37-year-old DIY blogger living in Krasnodar, Russia. He designs a variety of colorful projects, but wooden toys are his favorite. His son, Ilya, is a big fan of them too. Find more of Dmitry's work on YouTube at RadugaGrad.

Introduction

These one-of-a-kind wooden toys were designed with kids in mind—they're stackable, colorful, interactive, and tons of fun. Plus, they're durable and safe. I created these wooden toys for my own children, and I am excited to share them with you too.

The projects can be completed with a few tools and some imagination. As you move through the projects, you'll notice they progress in difficulty level. I've provided helpful instructions and full-size patterns to ensure you can complete each one successfully. There's plenty of room to add your own flair and personality once the pieces are cut.

I hope my designs inspire you—and that they bring joy to the children in your life.

Before You Start

The projects in this book are achievable with just a few tools, the first of which is a scroll saw—the star of the show! You'll also need a few additional tools, all of which are components of a standard workshop setup: a band saw for cutting the blank to size, a drill for adding blade-entry holes and different design elements, and a router or pneumatic drum for finessing the cut shapes. When using power tools that produce fine dust, always wear adequate breathing and eye protection, and work in a well-ventilated space. Tie back long hair and loose clothing for a safe and enjoyable shop experience.

When planning your approach to each project, consider acquiring a few premade details, which are staples in my toymaking work: turned pin dolls for projects that require people, such as the Rainbow Boat (page 11), ¾" (1.9cm)-diameter wooden balls for projects such as the Ravenous Hippo (page 17), and a thick dowel that you can easily slice up into simple wheels for projects such as the Car Carrier (page 14). All of these are cheap and widely available online or through woodworking and craft suppliers.

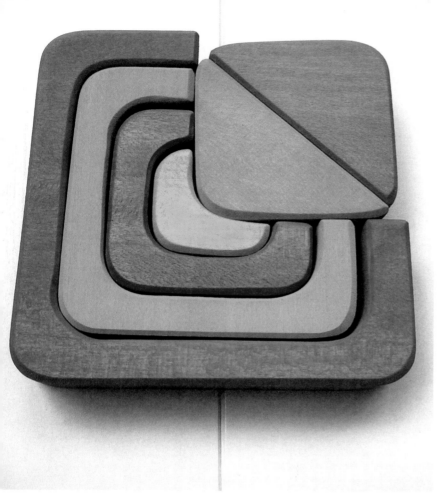

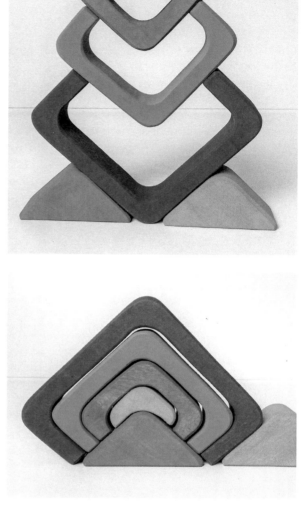

Simple Square Puzzle

This sturdy six-piece puzzle doubles as a balancing game

This little puzzle is a great tool for expanding children's imaginations, as well as their fine motor skills. Use it to encourage young minds to experiment with shapes and balance, stacking pieces in unique ways to create clever outdoor scenes. You'll be surprised by the wide variety of looks just six pieces can create.

Getting Started

Prepare the blank. I planed mine, but you could use a drum sander if desired. Remove excess dust with a tack cloth and apply painter's tape to the surface of the wood. Photocopy the pattern and attach it to the tape using

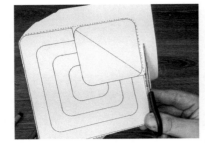

Cut out the pattern and attach it to the blank.

your preferred method; I used scroller's tape, but you could use clear removable shelf paper or spray adhesive instead. Orient the grain as indicated on the pattern, as grain direction and drawing alignment will determine the durability of the toy. Make sure to leave a small margin around the pattern lines, so each line is clearly visible throughout the cutting process. *Note: If you plan to make a few puzzles at once, I recommend making a reusable template to save paper. I use ¼" (6mm)-thick plywood or MDF. You can make working notes on the surface and store the template pieces until they're needed.*

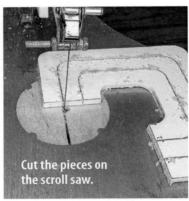

Cut the pieces on the scroll saw.

Sand the pieces smooth with a sanding drum.

Cutting and Sanding

Cut the pieces. I prefer to cut the small square on the side first, set the two diagonal halves aside, and then cut the four "stripes," starting in the center and working outward. Remove the patterns.

Rough sand the pieces. I smooth the flat areas on a belt sander and use a drill press with ¾" (1.9cm)-dia. sanding drums for the curved parts. You could also use a regular spindle sander, if desired. Progress through the grits from 120 to 180.

Soften the edges. I removed the sharp inner and outer edges of each piece using a chamfer bit in a router, but you could use a pneumatic drum instead. Then hand-sand each piece to soften the edges and surfaces further, moving up progressively through the grits to 240.

Soften the edges of the pieces with a chamfer bit in a router.

Painting and Finishing

Add color; I painted each piece with a different hue of color wax, but you could use slightly thinned acrylic paints, if desired. Let dry and apply several coats of a clear satin spray finish.

Materials & Tools

Materials
- Basswood, 1³⁄₁₆" (3cm) thick: approx. 6" (15.2cm) square
- Painter's tape
- Spray adhesive, scroller's tape, or clear removable shelf paper
- Sandpaper: 120- to 240-grit
- Tack cloth
- Color: acrylic paints or color wax, such as Biofa
- Finish, such as Krylon COLORmaxx clear satin spray

Tools
- Scroll saw with blades: #5 or #7 reverse-tooth
- Router with bit: 45° ¼" (6mm)-dia. chamfer
- Sanders: belt; pneumatic drum (optional)
- Drill press with sanding drums, ¾" (19mm)-dia.: 120-, 180-grit
- Paintbrushes
- Hand plane (optional)

The author used these products for the project. Substitute your choice of brands, tools, and materials as desired.

Pattern for the *SIMPLE SQUARE PUZZLE* is on page 20.

Towering Triangle Puzzle

Make learning fun with this freestanding five-piece puzzle

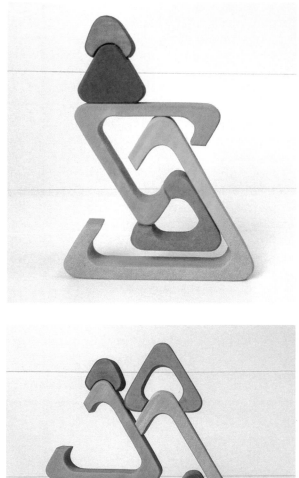

This curvy puzzle is a lot of fun to cut and color. Make a game out of how many ways you can assemble the pieces, creating optical illusions that engage the brain and eye. Children will delight in the many ways in which they can assemble the pieces—from simple and sweet to zany and off-the-wall.

Getting Started

Prepare the blank. I planed mine, but you could use a drum sander if desired. Remove excess dust with a tack cloth and apply painter's tape to the surface of the wood. Photocopy the pattern and attach it to the tape using your preferred method; I used scroller's tape, but you could use clear removable shelf paper or spray adhesive instead. Orient the grain as indicated on the pattern, as grain direction and drawing alignment will determine the durability of the toy. Make sure to leave a small margin around the pattern lines, so each line is clearly visible throughout the cutting process. *Note: If you plan to make a few puzzles at once, I recommend making a reusable template to save paper. I use ¼" (6mm)-thick plywood or MDF. You can make working notes on the surface and store the template pieces until they're needed.*

Cutting and Sanding

Cut the pieces. Start with the bottom triangle, and then cut the shape directly behind it. Continue cutting the shapes in order as you move toward the outer edge. Remove the patterns.

Sand the pieces smooth with a sanding drum.

Rough sand the pieces. I smooth the flat areas on a belt sander and use a drill press with ¾" (1.9cm)-dia. sanding drums for the curved parts. You could also use a regular spindle sander, if desired. Progress through the grits from 120 to 180.

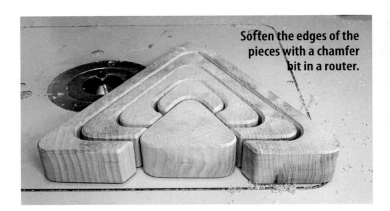

Soften the edges of the pieces with a chamfer bit in a router.

Soften the edges. I removed the sharp inner and outer edges of each piece using a chamfer bit in a router, but you could use a pneumatic drum instead. Then hand-sand each piece to soften the edges and surfaces further, moving up progressively through the grits to 240.

Painting and Finishing

Add color; I painted each piece with a different hue of color wax, but you could use slightly thinned acrylic paints, if desired. Let dry and apply several coats of a clear satin spray finish.

Materials & Tools

Materials
- Basswood, 1³⁄₁₆" (3cm) thick: approx. 8" (20.3cm) square
- Painter's tape
- Spray adhesive, scroller's tape, or clear removable shelf paper
- Sandpaper: 120- to 240-grit
- Tack cloth
- Color: acrylic paints or color wax, such as Biofa
- Finish, such as Krylon COLORmaxx clear satin spray

Tools
- Scroll saw with blades: #5 or #7 reverse-tooth
- Router with bit: 45° ¼" (6mm)-dia. chamfer
- Sanders: belt; pneumatic drum (optional)
- Drill press with sanding drums, ¾" (19mm)-dia.: 120-, 180-grit
- Paintbrushes: assorted
- Hand plane (optional)

The author used these products for the project. Substitute your choice of brands, tools, and materials as desired.

Pattern for the *TOWERING TRIANGLE PUZZLE* is on page 21.

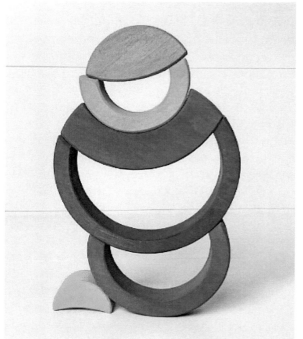

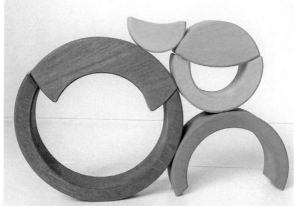

Layered Circle Puzzle

The sky is the limit to how many ways you can stack this interactive game

Kids will love to interact with this sturdy toy. It's a great tool for developing hand-eye coordination and creative problem-solving. For even more fun, you can cut several puzzles and intermix the pieces for a larger composition, such as the flower bouquet at right. I recommend this option, as it makes for a more interesting game.

Getting Started

Prepare the blank. I planed mine, but you could use a drum sander if desired. Remove excess dust with a tack cloth and apply painter's tape to the surface of the wood. Photocopy the pattern and attach it to the tape using your preferred method; I used scroller's tape, but you could use clear removable shelf paper or spray adhesive instead. Orient the grain as indicated on the pattern, as grain direction and drawing alignment will determine the durability of the toy. Make sure to leave a small margin around the pattern lines, so each line is clearly visible throughout the cutting process. *Note: If you plan to make a few puzzles at once, I recommend making a reusable template to save paper. I use ¼" (6mm)-thick plywood or MDF. You can make working notes on the surface and store the template pieces until they're needed.*

Cut out the pattern and attach it to the blank.

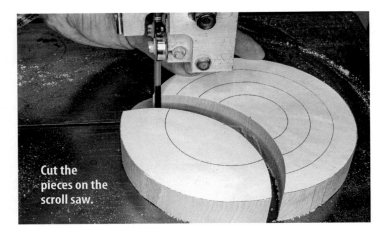

Cut the pieces on the scroll saw.

Cutting and Sanding

Cut the pieces. Cut along the line that runs below the inner semicircle, separating the puzzle into two sections. Cut the four-piece top section first, working inward toward the semicircle. Then cut the bottom section. Remove the patterns.

Rough sand the pieces. I smooth the flat areas on a belt sander and use a drill press with ¾" (1.9cm)-dia. sanding drums for the curved parts. You could

Sand the pieces smooth with a sanding drum.

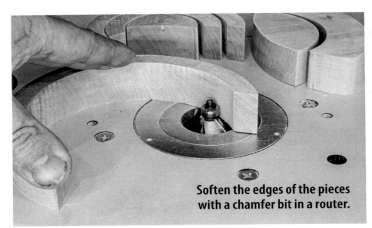

Soften the edges of the pieces with a chamfer bit in a router.

also use a regular spindle sander, if desired. Progress through the grits from 120 to 180.

Soften the edges. I removed the sharp inner and outer edges of each piece using a chamfer bit in a router, but you could use a pneumatic drum instead. Then hand-sand each piece to soften the edges and surfaces further, moving up progressively through the grits to 240.

Painting and Finishing

Add color; I painted each piece with a different hue of color wax, but you could use slightly thinned acrylic paints, if desired. Let dry and apply several coats of a clear satin spray finish.

Materials & Tools

Materials
- Basswood, 1³⁄₁₆" (3cm) thick: approx. 6½" (16.5cm) square
- Painter's tape
- Spray adhesive, scroller's tape, or clear removable shelf paper
- Sandpaper: 120- to 240-grit
- Tack cloth
- Color: acrylic paints or color wax, such as Biofa
- Finish, such as Krylon COLORmaxx clear satin spray

Tools
- Scroll saw with blades: #5 or #7 reverse-tooth
- Router with bit: 45° ¼" (6mm)-dia. chamfer
- Sanders: belt; pneumatic drum (optional)
- Drill press with sanding drums, ¾" (19mm)-dia.: 120-, 180-grit
- Paintbrushes: assorted
- Hand plane (optional)

The author used these products for the project. Substitute your choice of brands, tools, and materials as desired.

Pattern for the *Layered Circle Puzzle* is on page 22.

Stacked House

Unpack the possibilities for fun with this five-piece puzzle

This colorful puzzle is several games in one. Assemble the pieces to build a house fit for a fairy tale or balance them in gravity-defying combinations. You can even use the stacks to create a tunnel for cars (page 15) to race through. The possibilities are endless! The bottom edges of the house grip each other so you can lift the toy with one hand, transporting it from one play area to the next.

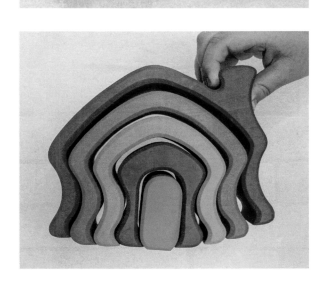

Getting Started

Prepare the blank. I planed mine, but you could use a drum sander if desired. Remove excess dust with a tack cloth and apply painter's tape to the surface of the wood. Photocopy the pattern and attach it to the tape using your preferred method; I used scroller's tape, but you could use clear removable shelf paper or spray adhesive instead. Orient the grain as indicated on the pattern, as grain direction and drawing alignment will determine the durability of the toy. Make sure to leave a small margin around the pattern lines, so each line is clearly visible throughout the cutting process. *Note: If you plan to make a few puzzles at once, I recommend making a reusable template to save paper. I use ¼" (6mm)-thick plywood or MDF. You can make working notes on the surface and store the template pieces until they're needed.*

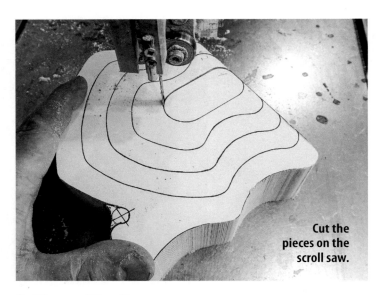

Cut the pieces on the scroll saw.

Cutting and Sanding

Cut the pieces. Start with the perimeter. Remove the wood next to the chimney with a ⅜" (10mm)-dia. Forstner bit. You can do this with the scroll saw, if desired. Cut out the inner door, and then cut the next stack. Continue cutting the stacks in order as you move toward the outer edge. Remove the patterns.

Rough sand the pieces. I smooth the flat areas on a belt sander and use a drill press with ¾" (1.9cm)-dia. sanding drums for the curved parts. You could also use a regular

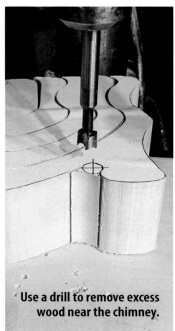

Use a drill to remove excess wood near the chimney.

spindle sander, if desired. Progress through the grits from 120 to 180.

Soften the edges. I removed the sharp inner and outer edges of each piece using a chamfer bit in a router, but you could use a pneumatic drum instead. Then hand-sand each piece to soften the edges and surfaces further, moving up progressively through the grits to 240.

Sand the pieces smooth with a sanding drum.

Painting and Finishing

Add color; I painted each piece with a different hue of color wax, but you could use slightly thinned acrylic paints, if desired. Let dry and apply several coats of a clear satin spray finish.

Materials & Tools

Materials
- Basswood, 2" (5.1cm) thick: approx. 5⅝" x 6¾" (14.3cm x 17.1cm)
- Painter's tape
- Spray adhesive, scroller's tape, or clear removable shelf paper
- Sandpaper: 120- to 240-grit
- Tack cloth
- Color: acrylic paints or color wax, such as Biofa
- Finish, such as Krylon COLORmaxx clear satin spray

Tools
- Scroll saw with blades: #5 or #7 reverse-tooth
- Router with bit: 45° ¼" (6mm)-dia. chamfer
- Sanders: belt; pneumatic drum (optional)
- Drill press with Forstner bit: ⅜" (10mm)-dia.
- Sanding drums: ¾" (19mm)-dia.: 120-, 180-grit
- Paintbrushes: assorted
- Hand plane (optional)

The author used these products for the project. Substitute your choice of brands, tools, and materials as desired.

Pattern for the **Stacked House** is on page 23.

Rainbow Boat

Rollable, stackable pieces team up in a clever contraption that kids will love

This rainbow boat toy is a lot of fun to cut and color. You can leave the body natural to show off the wood grain and then paint the rainbow segments with a medium of your choice. This sturdy toy is one that kids will love to interact with—from rolling it across the floor to stacking the pieces in different pleasing arrangements. If desired, you can scale the pattern down slightly based on your scroll saw's capabilities. *Note: This project requires a router. If you do not have a router, see Alternate Assembly Sidebar on page 13.*

Use an MDF template for production cutting.

Getting Started

Pre-sand the blanks to 220-grit. Photocopy the pattern elements and attach them to the wood with repositionable spray adhesive, making sure to use Template 1 for the boat body; you will apply Template 2 after adding the groove for the prow.

Mark the two drilling points for the wheels with an awl. Use the dotted lines on the pattern, a ruler, and a square to mark out the area on the top of the ship body where the captain will sit. Locate the center of this area. Indent it with an awl to create the drilling point.

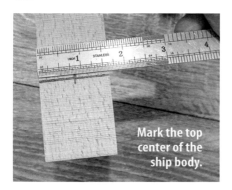

Mark the top center of the ship body.

1 **Drill the ½" (1.3cm) holes for the wheels.** I used a Forstner, but you could use a brad-point bit, if desired. Drill all the way through the blank. Then flip the workpiece upright and drill the 1⅛" (2.8cm) hole for where the captain will sit, about 1" (2.5cm) deep. *Note: Be sure to stabilize the wood in a vise before drilling.*

2 **Cut the rough boat body (Template 1), rainbow, and prow.** Use a scroll saw. *Note: For the captain, I used a premade peg doll. These are available online from a variety of sellers. The size of the hole for the captain may need to be adjusted based on the size of the peg doll used.*

3 **Cut the slot for the prow.** Using a ½" (13mm) straight bit in a router, slide the rough boat body across the router table, positioned as indicated in the sketched area in the photo. If you do not have a router, see Alternate Assembly Sidebar on page 13.

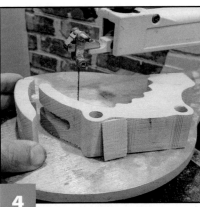
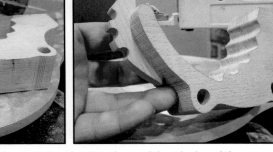

4 **Refine the boat body.** Apply Template 2 to the rough boat body and then cut it on the scroll saw. Dry-fit the prow in the groove.

5 **Make the wheels.** I make my own by slicing a 1½" (3.8cm)-dia. dowel into ½" (1.3cm)-thick pieces on a band saw. Drill a ⅜" (1cm)-dia., ⅜" (1cm)-deep hole in the center of the wheel for the axle. Sand each one smooth.

6 **Sand all of the pieces smooth.** Start by sanding the flat surfaces on the belt sander, and then refine the edges with a sanding drum, moving up progressively through the grits to 220. Chamfer the edges of the boat body, prow, and each piece of the rainbow using a pneumatic drum sander or a router with a chamfer bit. Remove excess dust with a soft cloth.

7 **Cut the dowels for the axles to size.** Lubricate the axles and wheels with paste wax and polish with a soft cloth. *Note: Make sure not to get wax into the holes in the wheels and at the ends of the axles.* Apply the same finish to the boat body and prow, let dry, and polish. Glue the prow in place. Thread the dowels through the axle holes and add the wheels, gluing the axle ends to the holes in the wheels. *Note: The holes in the wheels must be equal in diameter to the axles. The axle holes in the boat body must be larger than the dowel to allow for free rotation.*

8 **Add color.** I used color wax to paint the rainbow, but you could use acrylics if desired. Once dry, spray the rainbow pieces individually with several coats of clear satin spray. Apply the same clear finish to the captain, and let all pieces dry thoroughly.

Materials & Tools

Materials

- Wood, such as beech, 1⁹⁄₁₆" (4cm) thick: ship body, 3¹¹⁄₁₆" x 7⅞" (9.4cm x 20cm)
- Beech, ½" (1.3cm) thick: prow, 2" x 4¾" (5.1cm x 12cm)
- Basswood, 1⁹⁄₁₆" (4cm) thick: rainbow, 3⁹⁄₁₆" x 7¹⁄₁₆" (9cm x 18cm)
- Wooden dowel, 1½" (3.8cm) thick.: wheels, approx. 3" (7.6cm) long
- Wooden peg doll, ¹³⁄₁₆" (2cm)-dia.: captain, 3" (7.6cm) long
- Wooden dowels, ⅜" (1cm)-dia.: axles, 2 each 2½" (6.4cm) long
- Spray adhesive: repositionable
- Sandpaper: assorted grits to 220
- Pencil
- Soft cloths
- Wood glue
- Color: acrylic paints or color wax, such as Biofa
- Finish, such as Krylon® COLORmaxx clear satin spray (for rainbow, ship body, captain, and prow)
- Finish, such as paste wax (for wheels and axles)

Tools

- Scroll saw with blades: #3 spiral, #7 skip-tooth
- Drill press with Forstner bits: ⅜" (10mm), ½" (13mm); 1⅛" (30mm)-dia.
- Clamps: assorted
- Vise
- Ruler
- Square
- Awl
- Sanders: belt, pneumatic drum
- Sanding drums: 120-, 180-, and 220-grit
- Router with bits: ⁵⁄₁₆" (8mm) chamfer (optional); ½" (13mm)-dia. straight
- Paintbrush
- Band saw (optional)

The author used these products for the project. Substitute your choice of brands, tools, and materials as desired.

Patterns for the ***Rainbow Boat*** are on page 24.

Alternate Assembly

If you do not have access to a router, use the alternate patterns on the pullout and follow the instructions below.

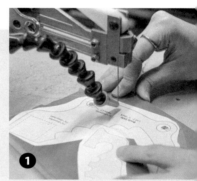

1 Attach the patterns. Mark any drilling points with an awl. Cut the boat layers.

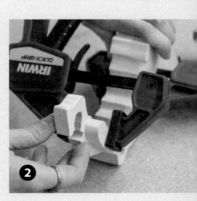

2 Glue the layers together—the outer layers will sandwich the middle layer with the prow. Clamp and let dry overnight. Sand the glued-up edges until smooth.

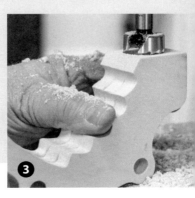

3 Secure the workpiece in a vise. Drill the ½" (1.3cm)-dia. through holes for the wheels. Then drill a 1⅛" (3cm)-dia. hole for where the captain will sit, about 1¼" (3.2cm) deep. Then move to Step 5.

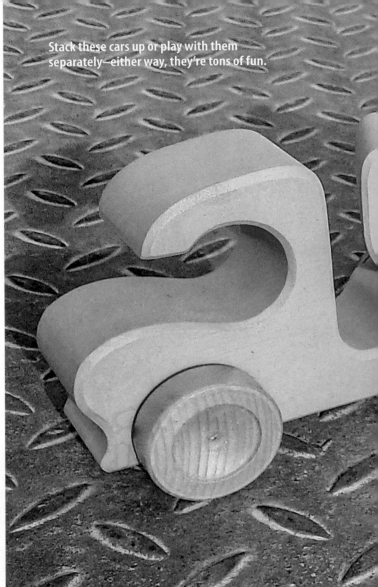

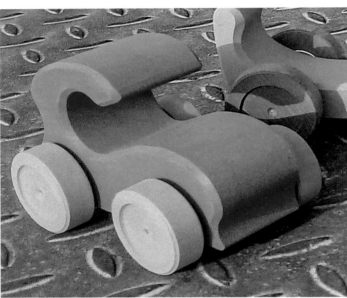

Car Carrier

This durable and versatile toy provides endless entertainment

This flatbed truck doubles as a puzzle and a toy! Stack and transport three cars on the back or zip them around individually. The cars fit comfortably in small hands and can be colored in a variety of ways. For even more fun, use the rings from the Rainbow Boat Toy (page 11) as ramps or the layers from the Stacked House (page 9) as tunnels to race through.

Getting Started

Smooth the surface of the wood; I used a hand plane, but you could use a drum sander or similar, if desired. Attach the templates to the blank using your method of choice, with the grain running horizontally. Then drill the holes. I used a ½" (13mm)-dia. Forstner bit to drill the holes into the vehicles for all of the wheels. I used a ¹⁵⁄₁₆" (24mm)-dia. Forstner bit for the large cutouts on the cars and a 1³⁄₁₆" (30mm)-dia. Forstner bit for the one on the tractor. *Note: You can cut these areas out on the scroll saw, if desired.*

Cut the pieces on the scroll saw.

Chamfer the edges with a router.

Soften the edges. I removed the sharp inner and outer edges of each piece using a chamfer bit in a router, but you could use a pneumatic drum instead. Then hand-sand each piece to soften the edges and surfaces further, moving up progressively through the grits to 240.

Cutting and Sanding

Cut the pieces along the perimeter lines using a scroll saw. Then drill a recess for the hitch with a ⅜" (10mm)-dia. Forstner bit. Remove the patterns.

Cut the wheels. Use a band saw. Slice a 1⁹⁄₁₆" (4cm)-dia. dowel into ½" (1.3cm)-thick pieces for the wheels on the truck and trailer, and a 1⅜" (3.5cm)-dia. dowel into ½" (1.3cm)-thick pieces for the wheels on the cars. Then drill a ⅜" (1cm)-dia., ⅜" (1cm)-deep hole in the center of the wheel for the axle. *Note: You can cut these out on the scroll saw, if desired.*

Rough sand the pieces. I smooth the flat areas on a belt sander and use a drill press with ¾" (1.9cm)-dia. sanding drums for the curved parts. You could also use a regular spindle sander, if desired. Progress through the grits from 120 to 180.

Use a drill to make axle holes for the wheels.

Use a wooden dowel to connect the truck to the trailer.

Attach the truck to the trailer. Insert a ⅜" (1cm)-dia. dowel into the hole in the back of the truck with cyanoacrylate (CA) glue. Insert the other end of the dowel into the hole under the trailer. *Note: The dowel and the hole in the top of the truck are ⅜" (1cm), while the hole in the bottom of the trailer is ½" (1.3cm). This is to allow the trailer to move freely.* Let dry overnight.

Painting and Finishing

Add color; I painted each piece with a different hue of color wax, but you could use slightly thinned acrylic paints, if desired. Let dry and apply several coats of a clear satin spray finish.

Materials & Tools

Materials
- Basswood, 2" (5.1cm) thick: truck, 3⅜" x 6" (8.6cm x 15.2cm)
- Basswood, 2" (5.1cm) thick: car A, 2¾" x 4¼" (7cm x 10.8cm)
- Basswood, 2" (5.1cm) thick: car B, 2½" x 4½" (6.4cm x 11.4cm)
- Basswood, 2" (5.1cm) thick: car C, 2" x 4¾" (5.1cm x 12.1cm)
- Basswood, 2" (5.1cm) thick: trailer, 2" x 10¾" (5.1cm x 27.3cm)
- Painter's tape
- Spray adhesive, scroller's tape, or clear removable shelf paper
- Sandpaper: 120- to 240-grit
- Tack cloth

- Glue: cyanoacrylate (CA)
- Wooden dowel, 1⁹⁄₁₆" (4cm)-dia.: truck wheels, 4 each 12" (30.5cm) long
- Wooden dowel, 1⅜" (3.5cm)-dia.: car wheels, 4 each 12" (30.5cm) long
- Wooden dowel, ⅜" (1cm)-dia., hitch, 1" (2.5cm) long
- Color: acrylic paints or color wax, such as Biofa
- Finish, such as Krylon COLORmaxx clear satin spray

Tools
- Scroll saw with blades: #5 or #7 reverse-tooth
- Band saw
- Router with bit: 45° ¼" (6mm)-dia. chamfer
- Drill press with bits: ⅜" (10mm), ½" (12mm), 1⁵⁄₁₆" (24mm), 1³⁄₁₆" (30mm)-dia. Forstner
- Sanders: belt; pneumatic drum (optional)
- Sanding drums: ¾" (19mm)-dia.: 120-, 180-grit
- Paintbrushes: assorted
- Hand plane (optional)

The author used these products for the project. Substitute your choice of brands, tools, and materials as desired.

Patterns for the CAR CARRIER are on page 26.

Ravenous Hippo

Feed this paunchy pachyderm again and again for endless fun

This hippopotamus is always hungry. It only makes sense to feed him—but kids will soon learn that he doesn't stay full forever! For added fun, position yourself at a distance from the toy's mouth so that throwing "food" his way becomes a challenge. Cute and interactive, this project will keep little hands engaged for hours.

Getting Started

Smooth the surface of the wood; I used a hand plane, but you could use a drum sander or similar, if desired. Attach Template 1 to the blank, with the grain running horizontally. Cut the perimeter on a band saw, keeping just outside the outer contour line. Then attach the patterns for the front and back Forstner holes. Use repositionable spray adhesive.

Attach the pattern to the blank.

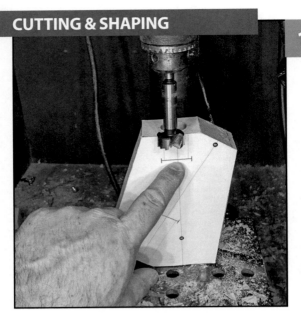

1

Drill the holes for the hippo's mouth and bottom. Clamp the piece in a vise and use a ⅞" (22mm) Forstner bit to drill to the depths noted on the side pattern. *Note: It is very important that you drill these holes before cutting the final hippo profile (Template 2), as Template 1 provides a flat surface for drilling on either side. Do not remove any of the Template 1 patterns just yet.*

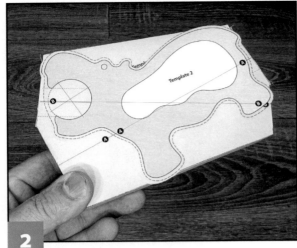

2

Attach Template 2. Use repositionable spray adhesive, making sure to line up the two axes on Template 2 with those on Template 1 under it.

3

Cut the perimeter of the hippo. Use a scroll saw. *Note: You could use a 1¼" (32mm) Forstner bit for the mouth, if desired.*

4

Drill the pilot hole for the stomach. I used the same Forstner bit as in Step 1, as it matches the profile of the front of the belly. However, you could use a smaller bit if desired, keeping to the inside of the belly perimeter.

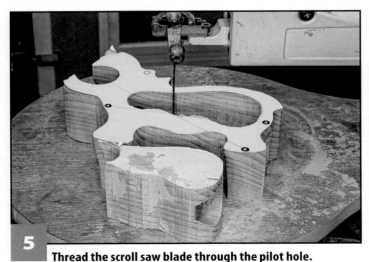

5

Thread the scroll saw blade through the pilot hole. Then cut the rest of the interior belly shape on the scroll saw.

6

Sand the mouth and belly. I used a ¹³⁄₁₆" (21mm) sanding drum, as it's ideal for rounded edges.

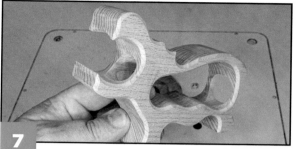

7 **Chamfer the outer edges and belly.** Use a 45° ¼" (6mm) chamfer bit in a router, taking care with the sharp turns on the sides of the mouth.

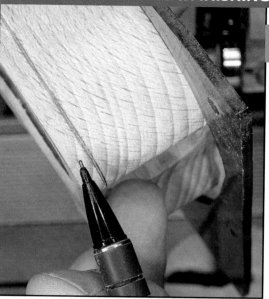

8 **Divide the hippo into layers.** I drew a line ¼" (6mm) in from the edge on either side from front to back. Carefully cut along these lines with the band saw so that when you are done, you have three cookie-like slices, with the thickest in the center. Use a straight bit in a router to cut a groove around the interior belly line on both sides of the center piece; these will create the recesses for the plexiglass inserts.

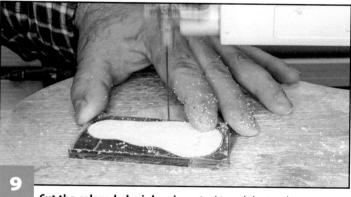

9 **Cut the colored plexiglass inserts.** I taped the two layers together along the edges with clear packaging tape. Attach Template 3 for the insert, and cut the layers on the scroll saw. Remove the pattern and separate the pieces.

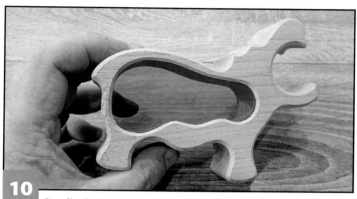

10 **Dry-fit the inserts and sandwich the three hippo layers.** If everything fits as desired, glue and clamp the layers together, leaving the insert areas unglued; they'll sit tightly enough as they are.

11 **Sand and finish.** For the rounded areas, use the same sanding drum as in Step 6. For the harder-to-reach areas, hand-sand, moving up progressively through the grits from 80 to 220. Make sure the bottom area is especially smooth. Wipe off excess dust with a tack cloth. Apply a food-safe oil finish to the wood surfaces, taking care to avoid the plexiglass. Add the wooden balls—I use around five.

Materials & Tools

Materials
- Wood, such as beech, 1⅞" (4.8cm) thick: 3½" x 6½" (8.9cm x 16.5cm)
- Colored plexiglass, ⅛" (3mm) thick: 2 each, sized for pattern
- Spray adhesive: repositionable
- Pencil
- Wood glue
- Sandpaper: assorted grits to 220
- Wooden pre-turned balls: 5 each ¹³⁄₁₆" (21mm)-dia.
- Tack cloth
- Food-safe finish, such as mineral oil

Tools
- Band saw
- Vise
- Scroll saw with blades: #5 or #7 skip-tooth
- Drill press with Forstner bits: ⅞" (22mm)-dia., 1¼" (32mm)-dia. (optional)
- Sanding drum: ¹³⁄₁₆" (21mm)-dia.
- Hand plane (optional)
- Router with bits: 45° ¼" (6mm)-dia. chamfer, straight

The author used these products for the project. Substitute your choice of brands, tools, and materials as desired.

Patterns for the **RAVENOUS HIPPO** are on page 28.

Patterns

Simple Square Puzzle
Pattern *from page 3*

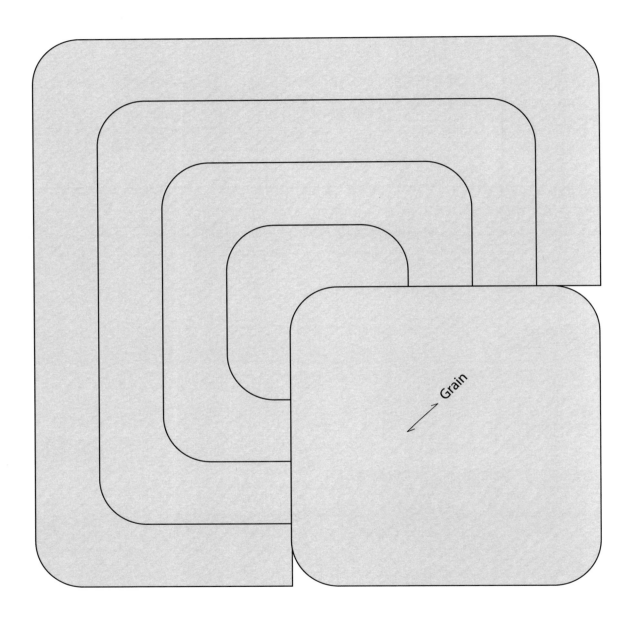

Grain

**Towering Triangle
Pattern** *from page 5*

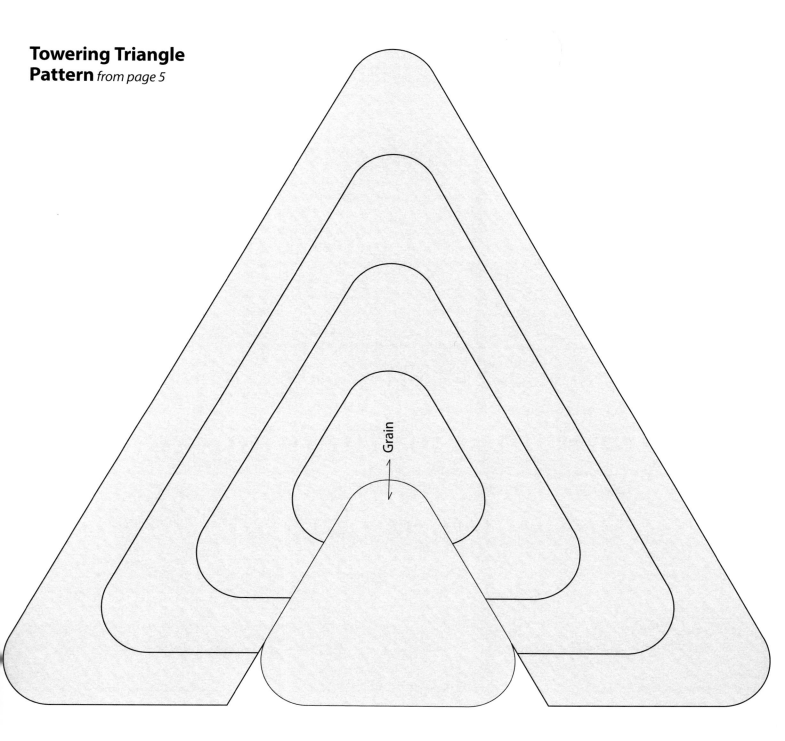

Grain

Patterns

Layered Circle Puzzle
Pattern *from page 7*

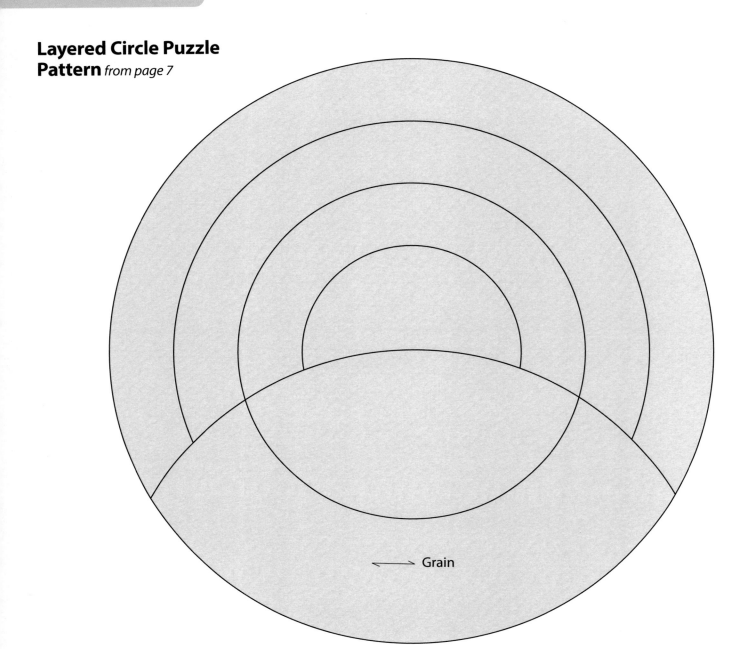

Grain

Stacked House
Pattern *from page 9*

⅜"-diameter hole

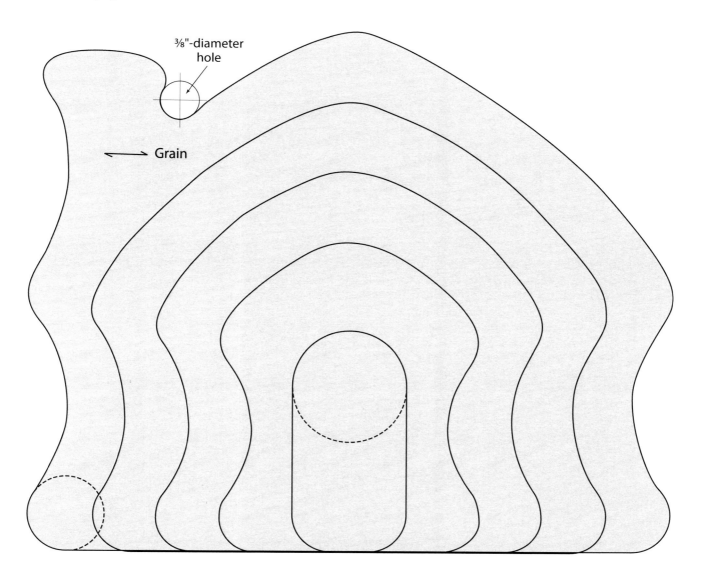

Grain

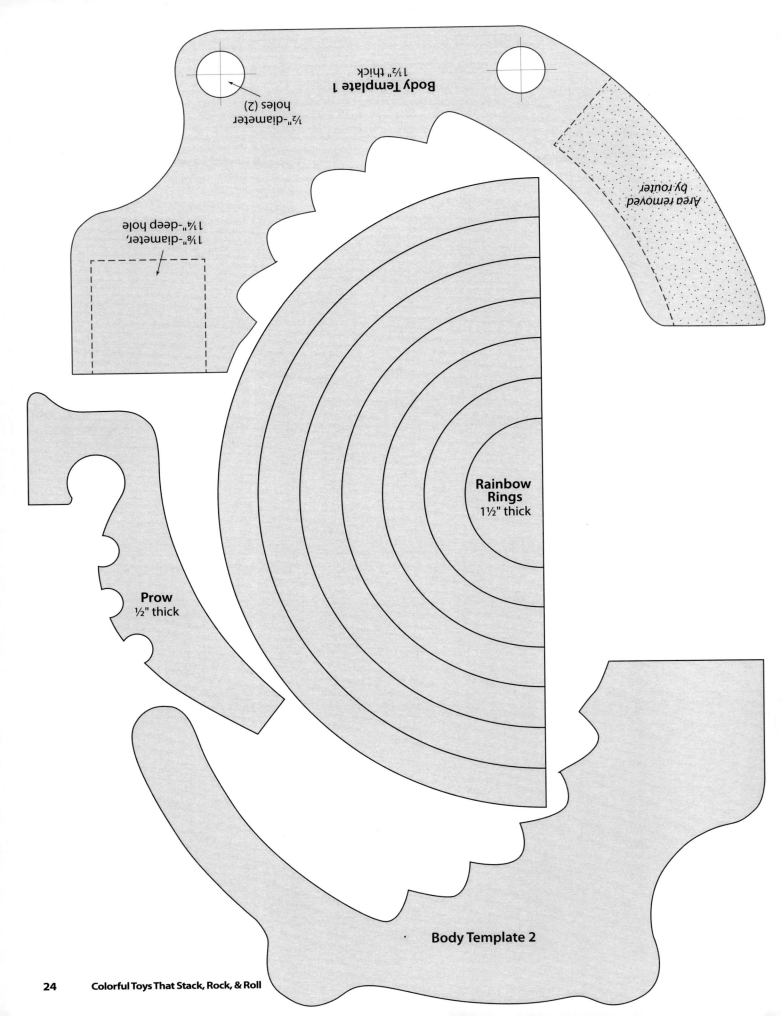

½"-diameter holes (2)

Body Template 1
1½" thick

Area removed by router

1⅛"-diameter, 1¼"-deep hole

Rainbow Rings
1½" thick

Prow
½" thick

Body Template 2

Patterns

Rainbow Boat
Patterns *from page 11*

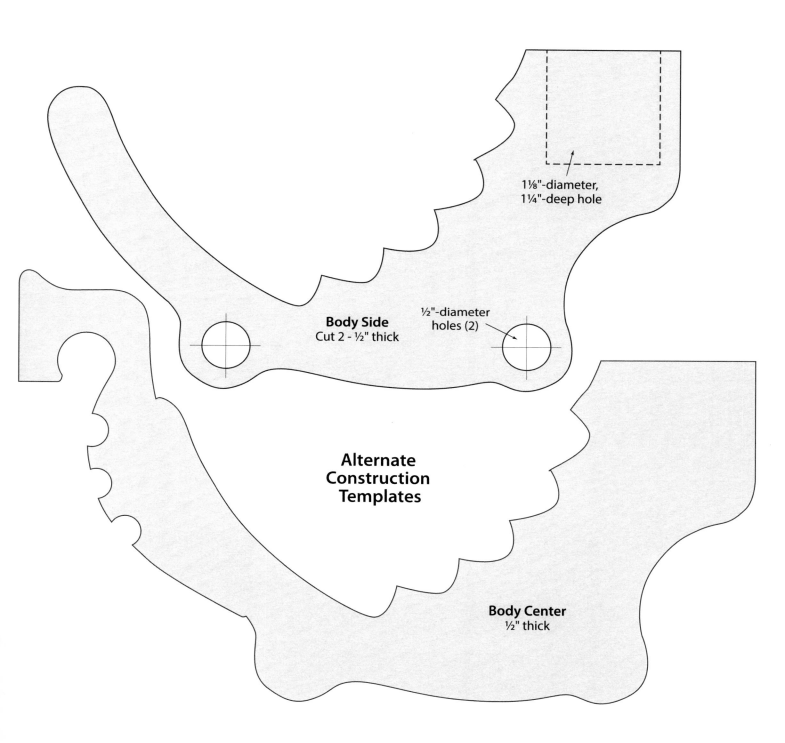

1⅛"-diameter,
1¼"-deep hole

Body Side
Cut 2 - ½" thick

½"-diameter
holes (2)

**Alternate
Construction
Templates**

Body Center
½" thick

Patterns

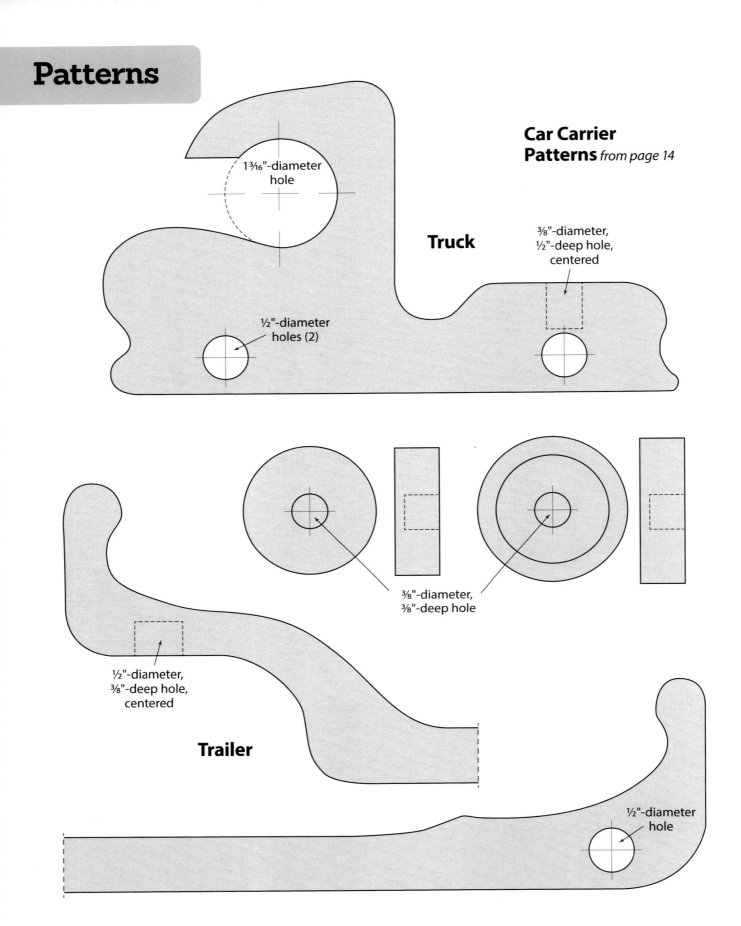

Car Carrier Patterns *from page 14*

1³⁄₁₆"-diameter hole

Truck

³⁄₈"-diameter, ½"-deep hole, centered

½"-diameter holes (2)

³⁄₈"-diameter, ³⁄₈"-deep hole

½"-diameter, ³⁄₈"-deep hole, centered

Trailer

½"-diameter hole

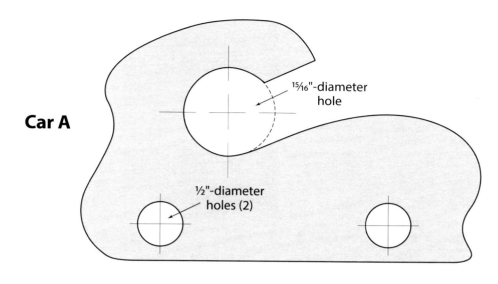

Car A

$^{15}/_{16}$"-diameter hole

½"-diameter holes (2)

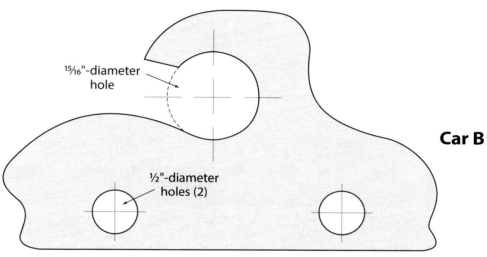

$^{15}/_{16}$"-diameter hole

Car B

½"-diameter holes (2)

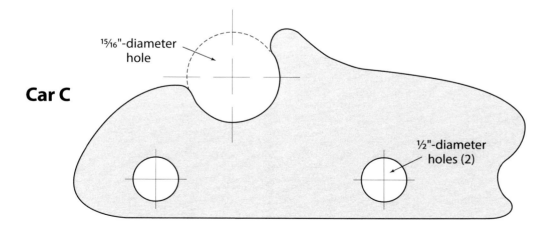

$^{15}/_{16}$"-diameter hole

Car C

½"-diameter holes (2)

Patterns

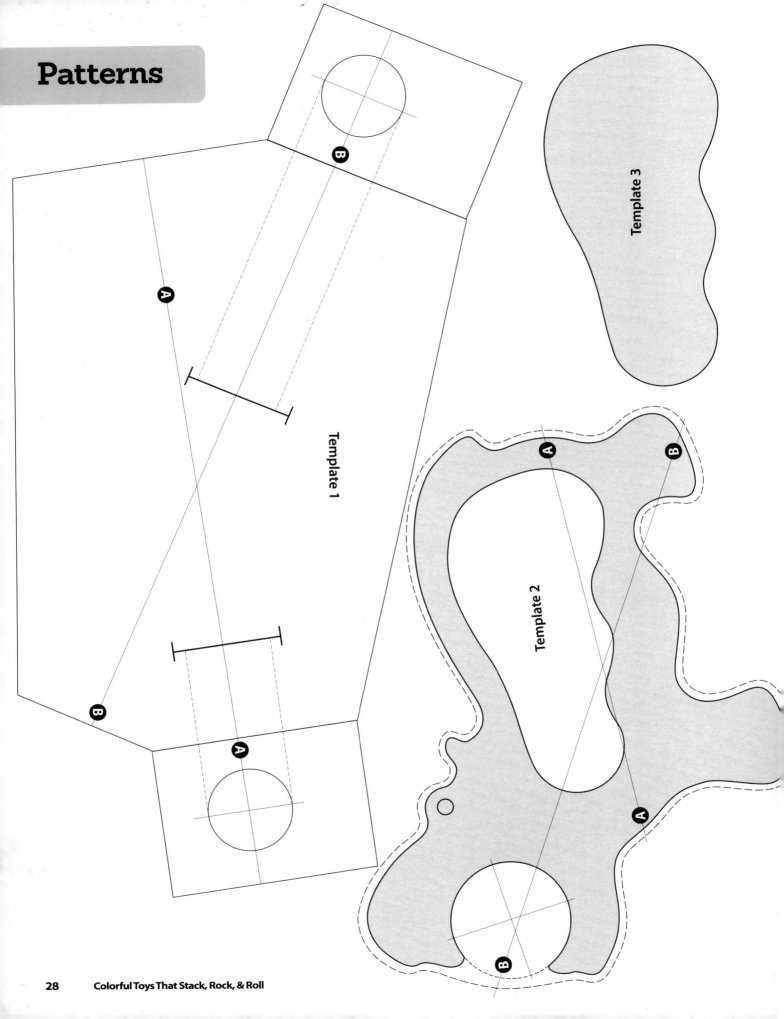

Template 1

Template 2

Template 3

A

B

A

B

A

B

A

B